THE PEACOCK TOME

SARVESH RAVIKUMAR

Made with ♥ on the Notion Press Platform
www.notionpress.com

The Peacock Tome

Written By Sarvesh Ravikumar

<u>The Greatest Enemy</u>

A fear is the enemy of one's life

That we all wanted to revise

All the words of honey, so sweet are the

Vengeance to which one and all leads

God once told us the pleasure, of giving

But never had urged us, for taking

He knows the worst happening in the city

And treats poor with pity

I asked for him a gift of pleasure

But he said that I had to do something special

One's life with compassion ends happier

One who curses ends with despair

My parents taught me a life lesson

About the facts god has spoken

To gain victory I must go far and wide

Sadness is just like the sea of tides

My heart, soul and mind know who am I

I continue my journey with efforts nearby

A happy starting here begins

And I'll fight for it till the journey ends

<u>Sonnet 720</u>

She was a snow who came into me, and left thereby

I never realized the truth, how foolish was I

Her hair was flowing through the west winds

Her beauty was the acceptance of all my sins

Something special in her that I see and I get

While seeing her gaze my heart becomes wet

Her dance was the great raining of petals

They fall to my soul where they all gather and settle

My mind is flooded with flying memories

I can't understand the fact that it carries

For years I've really been so sorrow

Happiness is the one that I should borrow

When I was sad, she closed my eyes

But what she deserved from me, was a mouth of lies

I was harsh and didn't know the reality

She was so kind to me and loved humanity

I owe her a great respect, deeply from inside

All her kindness stays in my heart where they reside

<u>Forest</u>

With yellow yarns tied up to high crowning tress

A greenish scenery that evolves with evergreen leaves

The mighty lions, in caves so dull

Where hawks all prey at a leftover skull

Climbers and creepers pave over my ways

And listen to the nightingale, what she says

Light above, is covered by dense, green canopies

Where footsteps land to the ground over dead leaves

Deer all brown, graze nearby the waterholes

Where there are small insects gathered by moles

When dawn arrives, the region is full of owls

As they search for prey in empty grounds

Bears all growl, while breaking a bark

And wolves all howl when the nights are dark

A lovely place to reside is seen through here

Lovely combs provide honey that they bear

The nights are full of strange, loud sounds

Made by elephants who gather in rounds.

<u>Peace Against War</u>

When time has come, there is an arrival of war

The knights gallop through the fields on horses

The heavy swords dagger a collision, heard from far

Blood strews at harsh faces, as all men charges

Revolvers fire at random heights and distances

Men in black against the men in white

Fighting athwart the dead sun's light

The sound of hooves interrupting the ground

Jacks against jacks killing with profound

A bravery act to be seen rarely found

A grave of peace can be seen at the last

Canons are weak, thereby the country is vast

Queens all spell the war to destine

Elephant are all anger, from the reign of regime

A cave of bones, hollow are bonded when cast

Heaven is always opposed to hell

Which is seen after conflicts when the men have fell

Beside volcanic fields all streams are red

While the men show no motion and are dead

Peace is the mate of life we all need to tell

<u>The Peacock</u>

Once a time in my fruit orchard, he crossed the shaded hedge

The feathery friend showed great beauty, all beside my ledge

Pretty feathers were dazzling with bright violets

A drop of one feather, seen with a keen silence

When the vermilions bloom, he was a flower as soon

His feathers were the dancing petals in a brief lagoon

He landed on my flower bed with a lappet of his leaves

He twisted his neck like a flower's bloom, on a soft autumn weave

He set his wings upright and thought of dancing in the rain

I got the most pleasured, happiness that I can't just gain

He was a male beauty, a gift of deity's creation

A feathery friend so far beautiful from my imagination

His color was that of a blue thistle

His neck was a violine of a sung, nice whistle

I have seen dandelions, but they were on his head

The peacock flew across my roof, where he led

He scattered his feathers in patterns and flapped his wings

Suddenly I felt a drop on my hand, and was the rain by winds

He was joyfully dancing beautifully on my roof

Off I painted him on my paper, which would be a proof

<u>The Paradise Season</u>

An autumn diurnal where the bright sun is high

An age where rabbits run and old leaves die

The snows all melt and the days are fast

Birds all chirp and the weary rains past

Graves all dry and muds all wet

It was new delight when the cranes all met

The falls wept down, and the please I get

The geese all swam across the stream

Cuckoos all fly across my garden all green

Melted snow covers on my roof

The smell of flowers indicates nature's proof

Horses all run through the west valleys

Their manes all fly with the dust it carries

How blue is the bright, sunlit sky

Bearing white clouds arranged by and by

Turtles seen nearby shallow swamps

They breed at edges, nearby flower blooming lamps

Here comes the dawn, where sheep all graze

The sun now hides with a dawned yellow face

Cows and horses turn back home

The birds all sing with a soft, bliss tone

The day now becomes too much dark

The sky is now being visited by larks

In my garden, the whole day I stay

Thinking about the flowers on a blissful may

<u>My Fascinating Reflection</u>

The oval, large mirror stood in front of me

Off I stood in front of my mirror to make a plea

My reflection had showed to me, my conscience

And I know what I have and who I really am

The plea of mine was not to just smile in front

The mistakes I make often gave me a very bad stunt

To always change the bad, the mirror supported

The mirror, of course me, which courage good I adopted

Finest huge glass was it's covering of the outer

It was between my good and the bad as a border

Often, I came daily near the mirror to just comb my hair

But every time when I see it, it tells me something with a stare

I was afraid of life when I looked at me in the mirror

It was pure magic which made me believe that life is not too farer

My aims are the keys to the doors of destiny

Lovely Spirits in my heart are stored in the kingdoms of mighty

To pass the tests of life, I must avoid the black dens of mischief

If not, we may never cross the life path, with great relief

The mirror said to me a great advice, who never ever gave

I trusted it honestly and now, know how to behave

When one sees his face, he sees his own profits and loss

And of course, head or tail of a coin that, one man has to toss

The mirror laments that I have learned a valuable lesson

Which I should learn to become a noble person

<u>The True Hero</u>

He had felt, the gloom of persecution

And he has experienced, the fear of discrimination

What he had seen in front of his eyes were dominance

Which had no big barrier like a quick silence

There was no gate against the rushing of violence

He had spent years in a dull dusty room of rods

Locked with floating memories of violent mobs

Against the blacks were the dominating whites

Which was like the ocean of very strong tides

Against the whites were the people in black

What they wished was the one they had, to take back

He was upset, but really so furious

To end the discriminatory policies had made him curious

Out he stepped his foot outside the prison

Questioning the happenings that had no reason

Off he started a struggle for peace

Which made the blacks live with whites in ease

He was a great modernizer of his own nation

He came up with a fact and that was called negotiation

All his efforts had made the country to live peacefully

This hero spent half his life in jail so really

He is one of the greatest leaders of Africa

And he is the one and the only Nelson Mandela

<u>Tomes That Preach</u>

The working of art all lie indoors of thy palms of hand

The sacred tales all crinkled, suspends writings all in sand

Words of despair, hanging with grammar all selfsame too old

Current poems, bearing literacies all rusty and life too bold

First, is the old dictionary, a mate of the language's lyrics

Second, is the prose of winter's cold and then autumn visits

Some accounts are about sacred history, and some of love

Where there is boredom, novels are thousands, and tells some

Bibles and Qurans are priested at edges with pages of holy text

Open to the counsels, gather the goodness, and turn up to next

Stories of musicians and tales of prince and princesses

Got mystery, got wisdom, got mighty within its white pages

Prejudice, distrust in faith with the group of wasted treasures

The final sort of tome is the ones that need us to face hardship

And there are booklets about the closest one, rather is friendship

There the ones about, fair relations and stories of affection

And finally, are the ones about the sciences of building brains

Thereby it gives greater knowledge, and serves to us all, gains

Reading pleasure does makes a king, or a queen, or an expert

Therefore, it gives the happiest, unknowing, greatest pleasure

They bear facts of life, soul, heart and sciences, needed to be met

Of course, yes, I would tell them are books, which all of us read

<u>The Greater Coucal</u>

She had a beautiful satin blued, mauve lined bill

As she hears the rattles and hisses, but merely no will

She lands upon a mango shrub and sets herself back

Fruits and flowers are not the ones that she eats, thereby lacks

She is an angel flying around the pleasure of twigged bushes

Sits on flowers, like on roses, but feeds on reptiles that she chases

She is a lovely fruit of orange, on with the trees

Earned to the sight, of her red lipped keens

She is an endearing one to me for I fed her with all my fish

She gave me a reward, and that was the most valuable kiss

She made a loud, blowing sound that echoes through the mist

This was a sign of calling me, as she loves me, and landed on my fist

She flew across the meadows, down the chairs of great nature

She sat herself on a white large rock, waiting for me to come later

I came beside her jumping around the fence wanting for her plea

The plea was surely bonded affection, that in her eyes I see

I went near her, and touched her wings with a waiting keen

But she starred at me with a dull face and sooner began to weep

I was surprised to see the tears from her eyes, and felt so deep

I wiped her tears with my fingers, but she still was weeping

She was in a sorrow mode I guessed and wants to lament some thing

She twisted her tail and flew to another rock and setting her beak up

Her wings were upright pointing towards the sky, up the sun

She dropped her orange feather on the rock sat by my shoulder

She showed up the sky where the birds like her were migrating faster

She kissed my cheek once again and flew to her crews

I stranded alone in the sand and sat with a well depressed pew

I took her feather which she gave to me as a sheer remembrance of her

And I would wait, stand every day in my balcony to reach her voice to hear

<u>Let's Take a Break</u>

If you need to take a break let's, go on babe

Let us dance near the buds of the autumn may

For she is like a spark, a dancing rhythm

Let us make a resolution, for this annum

If you need to take a break let's, go on babe

Let us dance near the buds of the autumn may

And it is here, the moment, for the taste

I am here for the taste, no time to waste

If you need to take a break let's, go on babe

Let us dance near the buds of the autumn may

Where Sisters all dance in the winters gust

And brothers all jump in the summers, must

If you need to take a break let's, go on babe

Let us dance near the buds of the autumn may

And if we all can play, no one is lame

With the coats all on, I'm dancing the rain

If you need to take a break let's, go on babe

With the gifts of nature, are always in vain

In the showers of winter, shall we play and gain

Let us dance near the buds of the autumn may

The Lemon In Water

Sinking in water but floating in mist

I am in the clouds sharing my pleasured wit

Green before the blue, flowing through my eyes

Angels across the barriers of deep blowing skies

Sank into the cold wet flowing ice, I am now disturbed

No more creatures but, for I never revered

Deep through the straws blowing all closer

I flew towards the life passing ice from future

I am cold as every admires drank the mist

I fell into mistress with a of a great dark cist

Flavors gone; I am a lemon floating on the crystal

The crystal is water where my pulps are fewer

Largeness of ice fall on to me, so harsher

They retreat through the end of glass, so further

Drank by vengeance, I'm now in a slumber

The straws wept down the poisons of temper

I am no fish but am struggling more, but to swim

I try harder with no regret, as I am no lemon to live

Struggles flew to the sky when the crystal has broken

With the flowing water I am now a true angel

The broken glass made me powerful, by kind

Pushed by the sorrows of my high settled mind

Straws now vaporize the cold streams flow

Sum shows agile between the ice no more

Designs all dance across my sun's west

If by chance there are no barriers still left

Paths are all bright, but where to go life

Ice or water, where no more, but were precise

I've gained from the lemon in water and on ice

Contents